DRIVEN BY DREAMS, JUDGED BY DELIVERY

Turning the tide for Belfast

Laganside Corporation 1989 - 2007

LAGANSIDE

ISBN 978-0-9555279-0-6

9 780955 527906 >

A catalogue record for this book is
available from the British Library
ISBN 9780955527906

Published by Creative NRG
Editor: Alan Watson
Design: McCadden Design Ltd
Printed and bound in Belfast

This book is the story of the success that is
Laganside. It shows in words and pictures how
government and the private sector transformed a
rundown backwater into the splendid waterside
development it is today, and how Laganside has
helped in the revitalisation of Belfast.

Laganside Corporation was given an ambitious
brief in 1989, against the background of 'The
Troubles' in Northern Ireland. It was set the
challenge to bring derelict lands and buildings
back into productive use, to encourage public
and private investment and to create an attractive
environment that would bring people back
into a neglected area through housing, social,
recreational and cultural facilities. Today, we
have a Lagan area which is alive and vibrant, an
area that people want to come to – to live, to
work and to relax.

This book testifies to Laganside Corporation's
formidable legacy of rejuvenating Belfast's
waterfront. The area's rebirth is symbolic of
the renaissance of the great city of Belfast and
Northern Ireland from a time of turmoil to a
time of new confidence.

David Hanson MP
Minister of State with responsibility for
Social Development

Anthony Hopkins, Chairman of Laganside Corporation (right) with David Hanson, Minister of State at the Northern Ireland Office, and Councillor Tom Ekin, the then Lord Mayor of Belfast, at the opening of Custom House Square.

I am pleased to introduce a book which celebrates the huge changes that have been made to Belfast's riverside. I was fortunate to have been involved for more than a decade with the work of the Laganside Corporation which spearheaded such a challenging process of regeneration.

Translating the dream into a brighter future

Anthony S Hopkins: Chairman, Laganside Corporation 1997-2007

Today I still marvel, as I did when I joined the Board of the Corporation in 1995, at the boldness of the vision for the rebirth of the Lagan and its environs, brought forth at a time of dreadful decline and hopelessness in our society.

I believe this book will remind many of its readers of the journey which Belfast has travelled over the past 18 years, prompting recollections of how things were then and contrasting those with the bright and cheerful place which we now call Laganside.

For those too young to recall what Belfast was like before all this began I hope our story will encourage them to nurture their civic heritage and to take pride in their fine, re-born capital city as it goes from strength to strength in the future.

All of those involved in this process of regeneration, from the earliest visionaries to those still turning the dream into reality, have been privileged to contribute to a rebirth of the Lagan and indeed of Belfast whose lifeblood the river originally was and is becoming again today.

Although the team in Laganside Corporation itself has been a compact one, with fewer than two dozen staff and a Board of ten, we have been part of a vast array of contributors - public and private,

corporate and individual, government and community - who have made this project succeed.

Some of the most important partners in this journey have included the Department of Social Development - our sponsoring department, Belfast City Council and Belfast Harbour Commissioners, each of which has played an enormous role in translating the overall plan into what we see today.

Everyone who had a part to play has a sense of accomplishment and pride in seeing how Belfast has blossomed over the years and all of them, I believe, share my view that this is just the beginning, a platform on which an even brighter and more prosperous future will be built for this reawakening European city.

As Laganside Corporation came to the end of its life it seemed fitting to try to capture the sense of change and to highlight, in pictures and in words, how the Laganside regeneration has altered the way people feel about their city, its standing and, indeed, their place in it.

Tony Hopkins

In 1989 when the Laganside Corporation was brought into being by an order of Parliament, Belfast was a darker and less hopeful city than it is today in the early, optimistic years of a new millennium.

The story...so far

Alan Watson

Throughout the 1970s and into the 1980s political violence was having a debilitating effect on the social, cultural and economic life of our capital city and the rest of Northern Ireland. Belfast had been forced on the defensive – with physical barriers that deterred everyone, not just those intent on harm.

With traditional industry long since in decline, unemployment was over 20% and international efforts by the Industrial Development Board for Northern Ireland to attract much-needed inward investment were being thwarted by global television images of a region seemingly ungovernable and intent on its own destruction.

On the River Lagan those who cared to glance over the Queen's Bridge were met with a vista of grey water, coal quays and scrap yards.

In the latter part of the 1980s, despite continuing violence, increasing attention was being given by senior Civil Service policymakers to the idea of a major regeneration of inner city Belfast. The focus was on the large areas of derelict and unused land around the Lagan. The Government commissioned a concept plan from Shepheard Epstein Hunter and Building Design Partnership. Its authors, Peter Hunter and Roy Adams, produced a vision to transform not just the environment of a large part of the city but the international perception of Belfast itself.

The plan was launched in March 1987 but a new body was needed to carry through the vision. Direct Rule ministers Chris Patten and Richard Needham put their considerable weight and enthusiasm behind the Parliamentary task of bringing it into existence.

A Laganside Company was formed in the interim until Laganside Corporation was formally established in 1989 to take up the challenge of regenerating the designated area. The Corporation itself was only a small organisation and from the beginning strong partnerships were essential, at central and local government level, with major land owners and locally with communities and river users.

Central government had the key supporting role. Through the Department of the Environment, and then the Department for Social Development, planning was managed, financial support provided, projects appraised and Ministerial support garnered. Another fundamental relationship was with Belfast City Council whose critical input included its delivery of an early and important landmark building, the award-winning Belfast Waterfront Hall. The support of Belfast Harbour Commissioners was crucial in the initial stages because of their extensive land holdings around the harbour areas.

LAGANSIDE

LAGANSIDE CORPORATION

THE STORY SO FAR
A RIVER RUNS THROUGH IT
CHANGING THE FACE OF BELFAST
BUSINESS COMES BACK

A PLAYGROUND ON THE RIVER
MAKING OPPORTUNITIES FOR ALL
THE ART OF THE POSSIBLE
THROUGH THE EYES OF THE WORLD

Laganside Corporation's first chairman was the Duke of Abercorn whose connections in business and tireless energy in promoting the Laganside opportunity were critical in raising the interests of property developers and initially sceptical investors.

Creating the right environment to attract private money required a significant input from the public purse – and the taxpayer has been handsomely rewarded. For every £1 spent by the Corporation over £5 has been invested by others, an achievement matched by few other initiatives of its type.

The phasing and sequencing of the key stages in the regeneration process were carefully thought through and planned – and the first priority was the infrastructure. European Union regional development funding was essential to making a quick start on these enormous undertakings. The EU provided money for a £14m weir which created an attractive stretch of water all the way from Donegall Quay to Stranmillis, covering up unsightly mudflats. New cross-harbour rail and road bridges were built, the latter helping to relieve cross-city traffic. Sites for new developments were cleared and readied. Lanyon Place was the flagship development, with the centrepiece Belfast Waterfront Hall acting as the catalyst to bring commitments from the Hilton Hotel group and from BT.

Encouraging people to live within Laganside had its early challenges. When the first apartments at Bridge End went on the market, Laganside Corporation had to run workshops for lending institutions to convince them that offering mortgages wasn't going to expose them to big risks.

Delivering economic and social benefits meant persuading major employers to set up shop. The early focus was on preparing sites such as the former Belfast Gasworks which had been left unsuitable for public use as a result of contamination from decades of gas manufacturing. With EU funding, Laganside Corporation and Belfast City Council transformed the area into today's thriving economic hub of national and international companies.

At Clarendon Dock, working with the Harbour Commissioners, a high quality environment was created for office and residential units. Elsewhere similar work paved the way for development, as at Mays Meadows. It was formerly derelict waste ground but became home to big employers, riverside apartments and a bar and restaurant. Public walkways linked these schemes together, giving unhindered pedestrian access to the burgeoning waterfront.

As Laganside grew so, too, did its remit and its ambitions. In 1995 Tony Hopkins joined

It is perhaps fitting, given that Laganside was born in turbulent times, that one of its final acts involved the removal of the last remaining security structures in the city centre to open up the area around the law courts and provide a key linkage from the waterfront area to the new retail-led development at Victoria Square.

1   2   1   A view of the undeveloped river corridor in 1989
         2   The city now faces the revitalised river

LAGANSIDE CORPORATION

THE STORY SO FAR
A RIVER RUNS THROUGH IT
CHANGING THE FACE OF BELFAST
BUSINESS COMES BACK

A PLAYGROUND ON THE RIVER
MAKING OPPORTUNITIES FOR ALL
THE ART OF THE POSSIBLE
THROUGH THE EYES OF THE WORLD

the Board as Deputy Chairman with the task of drawing up a corporate plan for the second stage of the life of the Corporation. His experience as a former Chief Executive of the Industrial Development Board and then as Senior Partner of Deloitte & Touche in Northern Ireland helped shape the strategy of sustainable regeneration which guided Laganside Corporation over the next decade. It was underpinned by a broadening of the membership of the Board, with Mr Hopkins taking over the Chairmanship in January 1997.

In line with recognised best practice, the focus of strategy shifted to integrating all the different dimensions of regeneration and ensuring that economic and social benefits were delivered to the local and wider communities.

A programme of linkages was essential in connecting the newly regenerated areas to the growing city centre through people-friendly streets and improved public realm. Custom House Square epitomises the value of open space in drawing the city closer to the river of its birth. Once a place where citizens of previous centuries gathered to hear public speakers, it had become just another traffic thoroughfare. Laganside Corporation returned it to the people, and it now hosts an array of events from street theatre to carnivals and fairs.

The Corporation's expanded remit took in what was previously Northside, renamed Cathedral Quarter, which is one of Belfast's oldest districts with a maze of small cobbled streets and some of the city's earliest buildings. Laganside Corporation's innovative approach to ending years of neglect involved the preservation of the area's particular arts and cultural flavour. The Corporation, for instance, purchased and renovated buildings to be let out at affordable rents to culture or arts-related businesses. New

public areas were opened up, such as Writers' Square in front of the Cathedral, and plans laid for a beautiful piazza behind. The public investment led to rapid private development and the creation of a lively, cultural focus to this part of the city.

To the east of the Lagan, on the former coal and scrap metal quays, emerged another landmark – the Odyssey Complex. Odyssey was built at a total cost of £91m, mostly funded through Lottery Millennium monies and private investment as well as a contribution of £9m from Laganside Corporation towards essential infrastructure works. With its 10,000 seat arena, cinemas, restaurants and nightclubs, Odyssey instantly became a 'must-visit' destination shared by all the people of Belfast and from far beyond – making it Ireland's most successful entertainment venue.

In and around Laganside were a myriad of different communities, many of them suffering from years of deprivation. Linking the social dimension of regeneration to physical change called for an effective strategy both to deliver economic and social benefits and to enable local people to influence change and grasp new opportunities. Laganside Corporation forged partnerships and improved communication with community and voluntary groups; and it developed an employability strategy to help unemployed people take advantage of job opportunities opening up in the designated area. These new approaches were a key component in delivering a fully-integrated programme of regeneration – ensuring what others have called 'audience participation'.

To create a sense of place and a new destination for the people of Belfast, Laganside Corporation put valuable effort into improving not just the fabric of life but also the enjoyment of life.

Its extensive events programmes on and around the Lagan played a key role in generating a buzz, providing a unique identity and branding Laganside as an exciting new part of the city which all could share.

In fact, ensuring that public places were shared by everyone was a key overall achievement of the Corporation. High quality public realm combined with public events, entertainment and festivals, built a real feeling that Laganside was a safe and enjoyable destination. Partnering with local communities, and recognising the importance of communicating with them, also helped foster an atmosphere of openness and neutrality. The lessons learned from Laganside are being picked up internationally as cities around the world face the challenge of fully integrating urban communities.

Laganside Corporation's task began with the weir and the rejuvenation of the river on which Belfast was founded. Its work and influence spread out from there but in 2007 at the end of its lifespan the focus had returned to Donegall Quay with the construction of the £50m Obel building. This 26-storey, futuristic tower of apartments is a testament to the new-found popularity of riverside living and a pointer to further development of the once neglected city quaysides.

The Obel tower reminds us of the scale of the change in Belfast. The transformation can often obscure our memories of the unpromising context in which Laganside was born. Certainly the project's success benefited from the improving security and political circumstances of Northern Ireland and from better national and global economic conditions. But from its

earliest days it also provided a glimpse to weary Belfast citizens of what the reward for stability and peace might be. In 2000 a report from the Organisation for Economic Co-operation and Development concluded that 'Laganside has redefined the sense of what is possible in Belfast'.

It is perhaps fitting, given that Laganside Corporation came into existence during turbulent times, that one of its final acts involved the removal of the last remaining security structures in the city centre - around the law courts - to integrate the waterfront with Chichester Street, the new Victoria Square and the expanding city centre.

Laganside today is a place of opportunity for all. Laganside Corporation's legacy, however, is not just in physical regeneration and the economic benefits that have rippled out through Belfast and into the rest of Northern Ireland but in the fact that the re-birth of Belfast as a modern European city goes on, with more ambitious plans for future growth and development.

This book, through the eyes of its individual contributors and through its vivid photography, tells the story of how, in the intervening years since 1989, Laganside has been transformed into a vibrant waterfront which has brought in more than £1bn of investment, attracted over 14,700 jobs, brought people back to live in the city and helped put Belfast back on its feet and into the holiday brochures. The recurring and inspiring theme across the pages is one of imagination, diligence to the task and the creation of a whole new opportunity for Northern Ireland.

	2
1	
	3

1 Art rises over Thanksgiving Square
2 Artist's impression of the Obel Tower development
3 Lanyon Place - a new city address

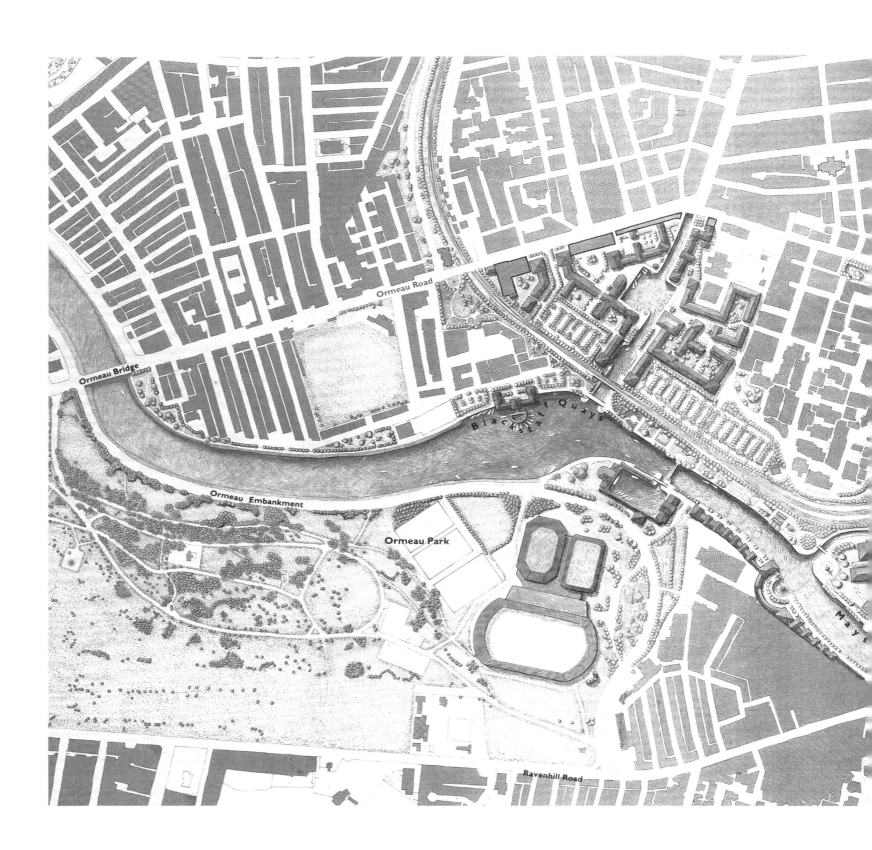

1   The original concept plan for the Laganside area

LAGANSIDE CORPORATION

THE STORY SO FAR
A RIVER RUNS THROUGH IT
CHANGING THE FACE OF BELFAST
BUSINESS COMES BACK

A PLAYGROUND ON THE RIVER
MAKING OPPORTUNITIES FOR ALL
THE ART OF THE POSSIBLE
THROUGH THE EYES OF THE WORLD

A river runs through it

Charlie Warmington

Carved way back in the history of time, the River Lagan was the foundation for the city of Belfast. Years later, when its usefulness had faded, it was almost forgotten by the inhabitants of Belfast until the Laganside project brought new life to the water and to its banks.

The River Lagan's main geological underpinnings have wandered around over the millennia. During the past million years they've travelled through latitudes currently occupied by South Africa and Egypt.

The history of the river itself goes back to the ice ages and is at least one million years old. Years after the ice melted a proposal for a city was floated. It may have been a good location for a new town but it was beset by problems that even today pose challenges for engineers. Belfast floats on mud known as 'sleech' – a soft, estuarine, silty clay not unlike porridge and sometimes called 'reinforced water' by the beleaguered engineers.

Belfast's fearless founders were not discouraged by such shaky ground. They excavated the mud and baked it into bricks to build the city. The river that created the mud also created the industry. Ships, soap, linen and rope rolled off vast river-dependent production lines accompanied by huge industrial ventilation systems, pottery and tobacco. Lagan water produced steam for the pistons, cooled the machinery and carried commuters.

The inevitable downside of development was pollution. Stagnant tides, laced with effluent, asphyxiated all but the hardiest organisms.

One of the first steps in regenerating Laganside, therefore, was to deal with the river. Key to this was a major infrastructure programme, the Lagan Weir. Costing £14 million, the 'space age' computerised weir, with its footbridge and service tunnel, is composed of five steel gates, each 20 metres wide, 4.5 metres high and weighing 32 tons. It ensures mudflats are covered at every stage of the tide and also acts as a tidal barrage to protect the city from flooding.

Water quality was improved by an innovative river aeration system and by systematic dredging to remove polluted sediment. A return of the natives ensued – animal, vegetable and human.

The weir, completed in 1994, is anchored with two underground concrete chambers of cavernous proportions and a line of 30 metre piles deep into the riverbed.

It has transformed the river and its surroundings. The aeration system pumps billions of bubbles of life-giving air into the river every day helping to mix fresh and salt water. The former Belfast gasworks and its river frontage is one dramatic example of new life. Now a wildfowl reserve fronting sleek new buildings, the district was once pungent and polluted.

Today there is 'wind in the willows' – and 'rings of bright water' denote shoals of rising grey mullet. The weir allows migratory fish to pass and gives leisure boats easy access to the upper stretches of the river. About 20,000 waterborne tourists on the Lagan Boat Company's 'MV Joyce Too' annually gaze on half a hundred riverside highlights where barges once carried thousands of tons of produce through the locks. Runners jog on these memory banks, on a

LAGANSIDE CORPORATION

THE STORY SO FAR
A RIVER RUNS THROUGH IT
CHANGING THE FACE OF BELFAST
BUSINESS COMES BACK

A PLAYGROUND ON THE RIVER
MAKING OPPORTUNITIES FOR ALL
THE ART OF THE POSSIBLE
THROUGH THE EYES OF THE WORLD

Belfast already has plenty of symbols. Many of them, such as the peace line, the security barriers and the army lookout towers project negative images. The weir on the other hand in association with other projects such as the new concert hall and the redevelopment of the gasworks site, illustrates what can be achieved when people unite to build for the future.

Irish News Editorial, 25 March 1994, on Opening of the Lagan Weir

1   2   1 A model of the proposed weir system is tested
2 The weir during construction

LAGANSIDE CORPORATION

THE STORY SO FAR
A RIVER RUNS THROUGH IT
CHANGING THE FACE OF BELFAST
BUSINESS COMES BACK

A PLAYGROUND ON THE RIVER
MAKING OPPORTUNITIES FOR ALL
THE ART OF THE POSSIBLE
THROUGH THE EYES OF THE WORLD

tow path that is a horizontal Tower of Babel with constant streams of maritime jay-walkers speaking every known tongue. Tourists lap up the history. The story of how the Duke of Wellington's mother, Lady Anna Mornington, tended her garden in a riverside dale (Anna's Dale) impassions the French. The 'Van Gogh' Bascule bridge impresses the Dutch, as does Lagan Legacy's 600 ton Dutch barge with its cargo of culture.

The 'Joyce Too' carries glitzy corporate parties, floating film shows, music, drama and romantic wedding anniversaries. She'll pass the nostalgically named Horsey Hill, Haulers Way and Potter's Quay pausing for thought, or whatever, near the river's popular drinking establishments - Cutter's Wharf, the Edge and bars near Queen's University.

Expensive riverside dwellings are now much sought after. All sorts of fish, birds, animals and plants heartily confirm the Lagan as a river of life. Abundant seals chase abundant salmon. Sculptural Grey Herons line the stone-faced river banks and angle for eels. Kingfishers, Moorhens, Dabchicks and Mallard make up some of the two dozen returned bird species.

The weir serves up their menu, controlling the water that brought back the fish; a success story warmly illustrated by little children squealing with delight at a glistening crab dangling on a string. Two decades ago all they might have caught was germs.

1   The completed Lagan Weir - breathing new life into the river

LAGANSIDE CORPORATION

THE STORY SO FAR
A RIVER RUNS THROUGH IT
CHANGING THE FACE OF BELFAST
BUSINESS COMES BACK

A PLAYGROUND ON THE RIVER
MAKING OPPORTUNITIES FOR ALL
THE ART OF THE POSSIBLE
THROUGH THE EYES OF THE WORLD

1	2
3	4

1 The redeveloped Gasworks site is now home to the Radisson SAS hotel
2 Her Majesty Queen Elizabeth II is shown Laganside Corporation's achievements by its Chairman, Anthony Hopkins
3 Fish and fishermen have returned to the waters
4 Rowers now have one of the best waterways to practice their sport

This study describes the potential which exists to transform completely the environmental quality of a vital part of the City, and by this means to help transform perceptions of Belfast at an international level. The proposals of the study are visionary. They are ambitious in scope and concept but are also pragmatic.

Richard Needham, Foreword to the Laganside Concept Plan, March 1987

1	2

3	4

1   An aerial snapshot of the river and its city in 2004
2   The atmospheric tunnels that run under the river at the weir
3   Apartment living on the river
4   Maysfield bridge

1 Reflections of the city at night in the smooth waters of the Lagan
2 The Millennium fireworks celebrations enjoyed by thousands of spectators in Lanyon Place

Changing the face of Belfast

Peter Hunter and Bill Morrison

LAGANSIDE CORPORATION

THE STORY SO FAR
A RIVER RUNS THROUGH IT
CHANGING THE FACE OF BELFAST
BUSINESS COMES BACK

A PLAYGROUND ON THE RIVER
MAKING OPPORTUNITIES FOR ALL
THE ART OF THE POSSIBLE
THROUGH THE EYES OF THE WORLD

Laganside would not have succeeded if it were simply about erecting modern buildings. To produce an environment in which people wanted to work, live and be entertained the planning had to ensure there were top quality public spaces as well as capturing the flavour of Belfast's maritime past.

The originators of Laganside believed that, if it was going to deliver its vision of transforming a large part of Belfast, the quality of life and sense of place of the regenerated area would have a critical role to play.

Experience elsewhere - in London Docklands and Salford Quays - showed that setting the scene with high quality public realm not only brought in private developers but also gave citizens new experiences and encouraged them to promote their cities.

It is the spaces between buildings that give enjoyment - or irritation - to everyday life. They form the character and visual memory of a city. For these reasons Laganside Corporation concentrated resources on building riverside walkways, enhancing existing public areas and creating new and exciting city 'addresses' such as Lanyon Place and Custom House Square.

Different design teams were commissioned for the various schemes but all were briefed to use the best quality materials that would endure and allow easy maintenance. Colour, texture, public art, lighting, signs and lettering were all aspects encouraged, and in some cases financially assisted, by Laganside Corporation. The lighting on the bridges and the weir, the Bigfish and the atmosphere of historic streets in the Cathedral Quarter all illustrate this approach.

The basis of good design was laid down many years ago. Sir Henry Wotton's treatise on architecture in 1624 defined the elements of 'commodity, firmness and delight' and these have remained touchstones for consideration of new buildings and development.

Today 'commodity and firmness' may be represented by 'need and sustainability' which can be tangibly evaluated and which form the basis for the initial assessment of development proposals. 'Delight' is the elusive but crucial element where architecture, art and beauty merge. It also provides an artistic and cultural legacy within cities - and it sometimes needs time and an historic context to appreciate.

Laganside Corporation sought to influence scale, massing and density of development as well as the quality of the external appearance and choice of materials for buildings. Local and international competitions raised aspirations and carefully thought-out development briefs were used to complete sections of the concept plan. In an unguarded moment, a senior civil servant described this Laganside approach as 'contagious'. It was meant as a warning about competition for future public resources but it may prove the ultimate accolade.

The rebirth of the waterfront, therefore, is neither accident of history nor the result of the natural progress of a city. It is an achievement of planning.

It is hard for any of us, let alone those born since, to imagine what the centre of Belfast was like 30 years ago when much of its fine heritage of Victorian and Edwardian architecture was being blown to pieces.

1

St. Anne's Cathedral, the centerpiece of Cathedral Quarter

The vision of a waterfront-led regeneration can be attributed to a few far-sighted individuals in the public service, given their head by a bold Minister who knew he could rely upon the resilience and faith of the citizens of Belfast and their elected representatives to see it through. Plans to build a weir to improve river quality, originally shelved as unaffordable, were looked at again as a means of enhancing land value and paving the way for developers to realise waterfront development.

The vision that excited the community was based on a simple sketch set in the context of a plan for the whole city - the Belfast Urban Area Plan published in 1989.

The implementation plan was equally simple - create a delivery vehicle to work with the principal landowners in preparing development briefs and give it money to spend on the public realm and to promote landmark projects. Public funding was made available for the weir and cross harbour bridges that opened up the harbour lands. Then Belfast City Council weighed in with Laganside's first landmark building - Belfast Waterfront Hall.

As project after project came forward, Laganside Corporation raised the bar on design quality and works to enhance the public realm. Its townscape vision of planned linkages to the city centre has

become a reality as the central city now spans the river. Laganside has also conserved and enhanced the old town on the north side of the city centre - another aspiration of the Belfast Urban Area Plan that would not have happened without a delivery vehicle.

Laganside was never about sweeping all before it into the sea and beginning again. The link from the past to the present was important in re-creating the feel of a riverside area. Careful work went into preserving and restoring its built heritage - including well-known landmarks such as Clarendon Buildings, the Custom House, the leaning Albert Clock, the McCausland building that is now Malmaison, the old Gas Office, the Meter House, the popular St. George's Market and - as Laganside Corporation was to discover - the city's oldest building, now the buzzing McHugh's Bar, which in its earliest days had sat alongside what was then the quayside.

But whether new developments or restorations, the lesson is that it is projects - not plans - that deliver regeneration. The Belfast Urban Area Plan 1989 pointed the way forward at a crucial time but Laganside Corporation will be remembered as having delivered the promised regeneration of this part of Belfast.

LAGANSIDE CORPORATION

THE STORY SO FAR
A RIVER RUNS THROUGH IT
CHANGING THE FACE OF BELFAST
BUSINESS COMES BACK

A PLAYGROUND ON THE RIVER
MAKING OPPORTUNITIES FOR ALL
THE ART OF THE POSSIBLE
THROUGH THE EYES OF THE WORLD

1 Excavation work at Four Corners in Cathedral Quarter
2 Building work in 2003 around the water feature at the Gasworks
3 Development work continues in 2007 with the foundations for the Obel Tower

Over the years INTA has counted numerous times on Laganside
Corporation's superior experience in urban regeneration. During our Annual
Congress in October 2006, INTA's members and partners from some 40
countries were able to experience how the once neglected area along the
River Lagan has revived since the last time they visited Belfast in 1991.

Michel Sudarskis, Secretary General INTA, world urban development association

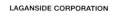

LAGANSIDE CORPORATION

THE STORY SO FAR
A RIVER RUNS THROUGH IT
CHANGING THE FACE OF BELFAST
BUSINESS COMES BACK

A PLAYGROUND ON THE RIVER
MAKING OPPORTUNITIES FOR ALL
THE ART OF THE POSSIBLE
THROUGH THE EYES OF THE WORLD

1   2   1 A bird's eye view of the waterfront in 2007
        2 The completed weir in 1994

With its 10,000 seat arena, cinemas, restaurants and nightclubs, Odyssey is a 'must-visit' destination shared by all the people of Belfast and from far beyond - and is Ireland's most successful entertainment venue.

1 2

1 Building the Odyssey complex and finishing touches as the roof is secured in place
2 The former coal quay is now Ireland's leading entertainment complex

LAGANSIDE CORPORATION

THE STORY SO FAR
A RIVER RUNS THROUGH IT
CHANGING THE FACE OF BELFAST
BUSINESS COMES BACK

A PLAYGROUND ON THE RIVER
MAKING OPPORTUNITIES FOR ALL
THE ART OF THE POSSIBLE
THROUGH THE EYES OF THE WORLD

1   2   1 European cuisine and a European lifestyle are now commonplace in Cathedral Quarter
2 Part of the revitalised Clarendon Dock, with a relic of the past in the foreground

1 Tree lined walkways shade commuters to and from Lanyon Place
2 At Thanksgiving Square a symbol of hope greets people as they enter the city

LAGANSIDE CORPORATION

THE STORY SO FAR
A RIVER RUNS THROUGH IT
CHANGING THE FACE OF BELFAST
BUSINESS COMES BACK

A PLAYGROUND ON THE RIVER
MAKING OPPORTUNITIES FOR ALL
THE ART OF THE POSSIBLE
THROUGH THE EYES OF THE WORLD

Laganside has made a fantastic difference to the River Lagan and its environs. Rowers now have a beautiful stretch of clean water to row on from the Stranmillis Weir to the Lagan Weir in the centre of Belfast - and as such makes training more enjoyable.

Richard Archibald, World Cup Gold Medalist and Olympic Oarsman

1	2	
		3

1 The former Klondyke retort house at the Gasworks
2 New business and life brought back to the area
3 Sunset on the construction of the Halifax contact centre in 2000 at the Gasworks

LAGANSIDE CORPORATION

Business
comes back

James Stinson

Once the home to much of Belfast's industrial might, the banks of the Lagan - come the latter half of the twentieth century - had largely been deserted by business and commerce. Today new investment has transformed the area and delivered economic benefits way beyond the boundaries of Laganside.

Belfast and Northern Ireland have come so far in the past 20 years that it's hard even for our citizens to remember what the city was like back then. Northern Ireland's traditional industries – textiles, shipbuilding and engineering – were in rapid decline. The political and security situation meant that efforts to replace jobs were largely in vain. Unemployment was close to 20 per cent and stayed that way for most of the 1980s.

Against this background the idea was formed that the answer to many of Belfast's problems might lie, at least in part, on the banks of the River Lagan. The thinking was ambitious but sound. Here were large tracts of riverside land close to the city centre lying derelict and uninhabited. They had huge potential – but imagination and hard work were going to be needed to realise the vision.

There was, understandably, some scepticism. Few government-sponsored job creation or regeneration projects enjoyed much success during the '70s and '80s. But 18 years later and the sceptics have been confounded.

The Laganside area is now a vibrant and central part of the city's cultural and commercial economy. Dozens of striking new buildings line the riverfront. There are offices, apartments, bars, restaurants. cafes, shops, concert and sporting venues.

The focus of much of this has been the investment that national and international companies have made in the area. By 2007, more than 14,700 people found work there, some of them living in the 800 new apartments that had sprung up.

Laganside and its new buildings attracted some of the biggest names in international business including Abbey National, Halifax, Hilton and Radisson - modern examples of commerce to replace bygone industries. It was also a magnet for new home-grown knowledge-led firms, including Northbrook and Gem, which exemplify the new face of Northern Ireland's business community.

Laganside Corporation undoubtedly hastened and increased investment in the city. It happened at an opportune time. People expected that a new prosperity would accompany a more hopeful political outlook and, as that happened, the world economy was picking up, too. Investors looking for new locations were now prepared be part of Belfast's rejuvenation – and Laganside fitted their bill perfectly.

1

Young businessmen relax in the cosmopolitan atmosphere of city hotels

LAGANSIDE CORPORATION

THE STORY SO FAR
A RIVER RUNS THROUGH IT
CHANGING THE FACE OF BELFAST
BUSINESS COMES BACK

A PLAYGROUND ON THE RIVER
MAKING OPPORTUNITIES FOR ALL
THE ART OF THE POSSIBLE
THROUGH THE EYES OF THE WORLD

As the Corporation approached the end of its life, a report from the OECD (Organisation for Economic Co-operation and Development) underlined just how successful the project has been, especially in delivering real value for money. By 2007, total investment in the area reached more than £1billion, four times that predicted in 1989. The £147m of public money invested through Laganside Corporation has been dwarfed by the investment from the private sector and third parties of some £850m. No other comparable regeneration project in the UK has delivered such leverage of 1:5.

The most exciting part of Laganside and the contribution it makes to business and the economy is that the process will continue. Private sector interest in the east bank of the Lagan and in Cathedral Quarter is buoyant. This latter area includes St. Anne's Square, a development of apartments, shops and offices

The Laganside team stimulated vision and enabled the realisation of many people's hopes for their city. The legacy of this model partnership is tangible.

Very Rev Dr. Houston McKelvey, Dean of Belfast

1   2   1 Assorted offerings at a bustling St. George's Market
          2 Cool and elegant dining at the Radisson Hotel in the Gasworks

LAGANSIDE CORPORATION

THE STORY SO FAR
A RIVER RUNS THROUGH IT
CHANGING THE FACE OF BELFAST
BUSINESS COMES BACK

A PLAYGROUND ON THE RIVER
MAKING OPPORTUNITIES FOR ALL
THE ART OF THE POSSIBLE
THROUGH THE EYES OF THE WORLD

behind St. Anne's Cathedral with a new theatre and a 200 room hotel nearby.

Confidence in the area as a place in which to invest and live was underlined by demand for the 182 apartments in the Obel Tower at Donegall Quay which, off the plans, sold out 48 hours after going on the market.

All the sites in the 200 hectares of Laganside have already been transformed or earmarked for development. And the impact on the rest of Belfast and the wider Northern Ireland economy is significant.

Laganside has paved the way for the Victoria Square development – a £300m shopping complex between Laganside and the city centre. Private sector plans for further waterfront development at Titanic Quarter, beyond the Odyssey, are as ambitious as those

Laganside Corporation itself aspired to almost two decades ago.

The work of the Corporation and its partners has helped change perceptions of Northern Ireland abroad, in sharp contrast to the days when the region was bottom of any investor's league table of places to consider. Today the busy waterfront with its successful, modern and growing businesses is as far removed as can be from the images that filled TV screens around the world for the best part of 30 years.

Laganside's positive influence on the economy of city and the rest of Northern Ireland cannot be underestimated.

LAGANSIDE CORPORATION

THE STORY SO FAR   A PLAYGROUND ON THE RIVER
A RIVER RUNS THROUGH IT   MAKING OPPORTUNITIES FOR ALL
CHANGING THE FACE OF BELFAST   THE ART OF THE POSSIBLE
BUSINESS COMES BACK   THROUGH THE EYES OF THE WORLD

1 │ 2

1 Building the Belfast Waterfront Hall, one of the first steps to revitalising Lanyon Place
2 Lanyon Place is now a place of business and leisure

1 2

1 Mays Meadow is home to corporate giants like PricewaterhouseCoopers
2 The river reflects the soaring ambitions of Lanyon Place

LAGANSIDE CORPORATION

THE STORY SO FAR
A RIVER RUNS THROUGH IT
CHANGING THE FACE OF BELFAST
BUSINESS COMES BACK

A PLAYGROUND ON THE RIVER
MAKING OPPORTUNITIES FOR ALL
THE ART OF THE POSSIBLE
THROUGH THE EYES OF THE WORLD

Laganside Corporation captured the essence of redevelopment for revitalisation - from an impossible starting point they have turned a dream into fantastic reality - and inspired the whole of Europe as a result.

CABERNET, Europe's Urban Regeneration Network

1   Dock workers offloading cargo at Clarendon Dock in years gone by
2   Building work begins to transform Clarendon Dock
3   The dock is now a major business district of Belfast housing many corporate headquarters

LAGANSIDE CORPORATION

THE STORY SO FAR
A RIVER RUNS THROUGH IT
CHANGING THE FACE OF BELFAST
BUSINESS COMES BACK

A PLAYGROUND ON THE RIVER
MAKING OPPORTUNITIES FOR ALL
THE ART OF THE POSSIBLE
THROUGH THE EYES OF THE WORLD

LAGANSIDE CORPORATION

THE STORY SO FAR
A RIVER RUNS THROUGH IT
CHANGING THE FACE OF BELFAST
BUSINESS COMES BACK

A PLAYGROUND ON THE RIVER
MAKING OPPORTUNITIES FOR ALL
THE ART OF THE POSSIBLE
THROUGH THE EYES OF THE WORLD

The physical regeneration of the city's waterfront undertaken by Laganside Corporation gave tangible proof to our audiences of the emergence of a new Belfast; a confident city, offering exciting investment opportunities.

Brendan Mullan, Chief Executive, Investment Belfast

1 2

1 Malmaison Belfast - an old building hosting a modern business
2 City reflections in the glass frontage of Belfast Waterfront Hall

A playground on the river

Ian Hill

Laganside Corporation's mission recognises the central role that events and entertainment play in breathing new life into a run-down district. It has supported a vast range of events that have helped make Laganside a place of relaxation for all and opened the way for the growth of a new, cosmopolitan lifestyle.

For centuries Belfast displayed scant affection for its lifeline, the River Lagan, which powered its foundries, mills, ropeworks and shipyards.

Laganside Corporation's task – if citizens and visitors were ever to stroll its banks, flirt by the silvery moon's reflection or make love in estuarial apartments or boutique hotels – was to reconquer the river on which the city had, for so long, turned its literal and metaphorical backs.

Sluggish and odorous, its mudbanks fouled with the detritus of the pre-affluent society, it would have been a foolish gourmet who sought to echo the choirboys whose once-upon-a-time perks were salmon taken from the Lagan's tributary behind St George's Anglican parish church.

But because of the port's success, the city's earliest, narrowest entries – found, as in any European city, between quay, cathedral and market house – had once been rich in Victorian oyster bars, Edwardian cigar divans, houses of high and low pleasures for skippers of Skipper Street, or winebibbers on Winetavern Street.

Behind the city's oldest edifice, the much-restored McHugh's Bar, beside Belfast's nod to Pisa, the leaning Albert Clock, had lain the raffish temptations of La Rue Plumet and Madame Du Barry's where 'Professor' Gilbert, brother of English painter Stanley Spencer, played barrelhouse piano for lovers of painting and other, sweatier, arts.

Who's to tell what novelist Anthony Trollope, once Postal Surveyor in the elegantly restored Custom House – which now overlooks street theatre, bounding fountains and circus festivals in a transformed square – made of such distractions?

Certainly new generations of novelists and painters, poets and playwrights, filmmakers and fire-eaters have taken Laganside's imaginative travails to their hearts, drawn in as the Cathedral Quarter's cultural concept seeded genes to its eponymous arts festival and an extended family of creative artistic Mammons.

Laganside Corporation's strategy was to make the area a venue for events to draw all sections of

1 2

1 Gourmet cuisine is the order of the day
2 Café culture and cobbled pavings in Cathedral Quarter

LAGANSIDE CORPORATION

THE STORY SO FAR
A RIVER RUNS THROUGH IT
CHANGING THE FACE OF BELFAST
BUSINESS COMES BACK

A PLAYGROUND ON THE RIVER
MAKING OPPORTUNITIES FOR ALL
THE ART OF THE POSSIBLE
THROUGH THE EYES OF THE WORLD

LAGANSIDE CORPORATION

THE STORY SO FAR
A RIVER RUNS THROUGH IT
CHANGING THE FACE OF BELFAST
BUSINESS COMES BACK

A PLAYGROUND ON THE RIVER
MAKING OPPORTUNITIES FOR ALL
THE ART OF THE POSSIBLE
THROUGH THE EYES OF THE WORLD

society to new, shared space and to help rebuild the confidence of the people of Belfast. Events as diverse as you'd care to imagine - from jet ski racing on the river to a rockabilly festival or the contest for the UK's strongest man - drew a million people a year to the waterfront on a journey of discovery and revelation.

One of the earliest and most important landmark buildings, the Waterfront Hall, brought the petit bourgeois to where their ancestors slaved for a pittance. Then came developers, as spin-offs from festival and hall rediscovered the catalyst to the ambitious commercial revival of the left bank.

The Lagan's other bank has its Odyssey with its multi-screens, superstar gigs, ice-hockey jocks, the W5 science centre, plus a panoply of ever-changing bars and ethnic eateries - and the emergent Titanic Quarter.

Transformation has rescued the city, and thus Northern Ireland, from centuries of industrial despoliation, decades of post-industrial neglect and the hardships of years of 'the Troubles'.

On the left bank, art students and their imitators, jeans rigged to current fashions, jaunt from their revitalised College on York Street down Donegall and Waring Streets, boulevards of decorated 18th century granite and stucco banks and warehouses which claim to be both the city's old 'Fleet Street' and its new 'Soho'.

They patronise bars - cool or retro - craft shops and brasseries, plus the Black Box Theatre, dreaming of their own entrepreneurial design, photographic, co-operative studio and gallery outlets.

Their ambitions - plus those of the area's cynical hacks, stylish architects, stripe-suited lawyers, wild-haired poets, modestly-salaried arts managers, combative playwrights and culture's louche observers - are the blood which rushes through the cobbled entries which in turn are the veins of the Cathedral Cultural Quarter.

Under the Lagan Weir, in squash-court like boxes, actors and artists flex their futures, their audiences keener on culture's alternatives

1 2

1 Cutting edge architecture juxtaposes with old red-brick Belfast
2 Gargoyles adorn the refurbished Albert Clock

than on Barry Douglas and Sir James Galway revisiting the classics up above.

Graduate students mix over lunch with business types choosing from menus proffering cuisines of a dozen cultures, served by nationals of another dozen to tourists from even further continents. They waft through galleries, cruise Laganside's empire by foot or waterbus, from the piazzas of Clarendon Dock to the gentrified Gasworks.

Come what used to be teatime, guys pocket ties, gals undo another button, before booking classic, country, rock or tribute Waterfront Hall concerts. In a thousand waterside apartments, thirty-somethings shower for an evening's fun. Car parks disgorge nine-to-fivers, filling up again as country comes to town.

1   BBC Music Live floating stage at Lanyon Place

LAGANSIDE CORPORATION

THE STORY SO FAR
A RIVER RUNS THROUGH IT
CHANGING THE FACE OF BELFAST
BUSINESS COMES BACK

A PLAYGROUND ON THE RIVER
MAKING OPPORTUNITIES FOR ALL
THE ART OF THE POSSIBLE
THROUGH THE EYES OF THE WORLD

Events as diverse as you'd care to imagine - from jet ski racing on the river to a rockabilly festival or a contest for the UK's strongest man - have, with support from Laganside Corporation, drawn a million people a year to the waterfront on a journey of discovery and revelation.

1 Nightclubs oozing sophistication
2 Up and coming artists display their craft to public scrutiny
3 Competition hots up on the waterways

1 2

1 A saucy girls' night out at the Odyssey complex
2 Lazy jazz beats on into the night

LAGANSIDE CORPORATION

LAGANSIDE CORPORATION

THE STORY SO FAR
A RIVER RUNS THROUGH IT
CHANGING THE FACE OF BELFAST
BUSINESS COMES BACK

A PLAYGROUND ON THE RIVER
MAKING OPPORTUNITIES FOR ALL
THE ART OF THE POSSIBLE
THROUGH THE EYES OF THE WORLD

Making opportunities for all

David Lockhart and Kyle Alexander

LAGANSIDE CORPORATION

THE STORY SO FAR
A RIVER RUNS THROUGH IT
CHANGING THE FACE OF BELFAST
BUSINESS COMES BACK

A PLAYGROUND ON THE RIVER
MAKING OPPORTUNITIES FOR ALL
THE ART OF THE POSSIBLE
THROUGH THE EYES OF THE WORLD

Social regeneration was critical to the renewal of the districts around the River Lagan. Working with communities became a central plank in the strategy and key measures were taken to ensure that people, particularly the unemployed, would have a chance to benefit from the influx of new investment.

As a local youth club was being shown round the Gasworks site in 1995 the Laganside planner described the infrastructure works, the funding strategy and the potential for private sector investment. One young girl interrupted him to ask: "Yes, but what's in it for me? What are you doing to make sure I get a job here?"

Her questions went to the heart of discussions within Laganside Corporation at the time. While local communities had been consulted on plans since the beginning, what positive action could be taken to ensure real benefit to local people? And so emerged a community strategy, a community team and community representation on the Corporation's board. The new mission statement sought to make Laganside 'a place of opportunity for all'.

The approach was multidimensional – engaging with community groups, supporting community events, ensuring provision of social housing, introducing equality policies to ensure equitable treatment for all and communicating regularly through the 'Laganlines' newspaper.

The approach was also personal. One community representative commented: "The difference with Laganside was that they came out to talk to us and seek our views." Anne Harty, Community Officer for over ten years, played an invaluable role in building positive relationships with local groups.

Creating access for local people to the many new job opportunities on the waterfront was perhaps the greatest challenge.

The economic health of communities is everyone's concern. Laganside Corporation believed that companies which located in the area had an important role to play in creating a more prosperous society through partnerships with a number of organisations dedicated to helping the unemployed in local communities.

These companies, in conjunction with others, promoted sustainable development by offering recruitment, training and employment opportunities to the unemployed.

In line with this ethos, Laganside Corporation's Employment and Employability Strategy focused on supporting the public, private, voluntary and community sectors in delivering employability schemes that enabled unemployed people access to the 14,700 jobs located in the Laganside area.

It was also instrumental in initiating and supporting Belfast GEMS (Gas Works Employment Matching Service) now GEMS NI, an area-based employability project covering south Belfast.

Susan Russam, Chief Executive of GEMS NI, says: "Laganside Corporation influenced the recruitment and selection mechanisms of major employers in the Laganside area in respect of Corporate Social Responsibility, taking it beyond 'corporate giving'. This allowed us and other similar initiatives to support significant numbers of long-term unemployed to gain jobs in Laganside."

1

Entertainment by the river brings joy to the faces of Belfast children

A Community Led Regeneration Grants scheme was also very successful and supported nine employability projects delivered throughout the city.

The specialist schemes supported by Laganside Corporation targeted those hardest to reach including the long-term unemployed, ethnic minorities, those with learning difficulties, lone parents and the economically inactive.

The engagement with Laganside employers helped community employability initiatives gain access to HR personnel and the job opportunities on offer. A Laganside employers' forum allowed companies to share best practice in recruiting the long-term unemployed.

Other outreach work included participating in relevant community employability forums such as LEAP, the Local Employment Access Partnership initiative in north Belfast, and the East Belfast Employability Working Group. Laganside Corporation also supported jobfairs that brought information and job opportunities to thousands from the local community.

The value of liaison work has been recognised by the employers. Bro McFerran, Managing Director of Northbrook Technology, identifies the working relationship developed between his HR department and Laganside's Employment

& Employability Team as critically important in engaging with the long term unemployed. He says: "The tailored pre-employment training schemes funded by Laganside proved very successful and resulted in many unemployed people gaining jobs with the company."

At the Halifax/HBOS retail contact centre at the Gasworks, Alison Thornbury, the company's Site Resourcing Team Manager, believes Laganside Corporation's role in setting up an employers' forum and working with their recruitment team brought major benefits. "They helped us take advantage of pre-employment training initiatives in the community which led to many previously unemployed people finding work with us," she adds.

Working with an active and initially sceptical community sector, without overstepping the bounds of its responsibilities and treading on the toes of others, was a difficult challenge. But Laganside Corporation knew that providing employment opportunities for people was central to the social regeneration of the area. By making appropriate interventions into the labour market it opened up access to training and jobs, bringing real value to people in the local community.

LAGANSIDE CORPORATION

THE STORY SO FAR
A RIVER RUNS THROUGH IT
CHANGING THE FACE OF BELFAST
BUSINESS COMES BACK

A PLAYGROUND ON THE RIVER
MAKING OPPORTUNITIES FOR ALL
THE ART OF THE POSSIBLE
THROUGH THE EYES OF THE WORLD

1   2

1   The Calder fountain in Queen's Square restored to its former glory
2   Business booms with young talent

78.79

LAGANSIDE CORPORATION

THE STORY SO FAR
A RIVER RUNS THROUGH IT
CHANGING THE FACE OF BELFAST
BUSINESS COMES BACK

A PLAYGROUND ON THE RIVER
MAKING OPPORTUNITIES FOR ALL
THE ART OF THE POSSIBLE
THROUGH THE EYES OF THE WORLD

Laganside Corporation influenced the recruitment and selection mechanisms of major employers in the Laganside area in respect of Corporate Social Responsibility, taking it beyond 'corporate giving'. This allowed us and other similar initiatives to support significant numbers of long-term unemployed to gain jobs in Laganside.

Susan Russam, GEMS NI

1   2

1 Colourful riverside apartments are today's must-have addresses
2 Art brings community and business together

LAGANSIDE CORPORATION

THE STORY SO FAR
A RIVER RUNS THROUGH IT
CHANGING THE FACE OF BELFAST
BUSINESS COMES BACK

A PLAYGROUND ON THE RIVER
MAKING OPPORTUNITIES FOR ALL
THE ART OF THE POSSIBLE
THROUGH THE EYES OF THE WORLD

1   2

1   Energetically making waves on the river
2   Laganside Courts - illuminating the law

1 Skylight apertures flood workers with light
2 Burly Belfast Giants enthral the Odyssey Arena crowds
3 Business men relax in comfort and style at the Hilton Hotel

LAGANSIDE CORPORATION

THE STORY SO FAR
A RIVER RUNS THROUGH IT
CHANGING THE FACE OF BELFAST
BUSINESS COMES BACK

A PLAYGROUND ON THE RIVER
MAKING OPPORTUNITIES FOR ALL
THE ART OF THE POSSIBLE
THROUGH THE EYES OF THE WORLD

Wonderful artworks, beautiful bridges,
boats, seals, fish - all from our windows.
How lucky we are.

Winnie and Bob Strang, residents of Gregg's Quay

1 | 2

1 Music and comedy combine at arts festivals across the city
2 Hip hotels welcome the weary traveller

LAGANSIDE CORPORATION

THE STORY SO FAR
A RIVER RUNS THROUGH IT
CHANGING THE FACE OF BELFAST
BUSINESS COMES BACK

A PLAYGROUND ON THE RIVER
MAKING OPPORTUNITIES FOR ALL
THE ART OF THE POSSIBLE
THROUGH THE EYES OF THE WORLD

The art of the possible

Jane Coyle

An important element
of Laganside's regeneration
was the linking of the past,
present and future. By
commissioning more than 30
pieces of public art, Laganside
Corporation was mindful of
an important heritage. Public
art has added to the cultural
richness of Belfast and given
focus to many of the area's
open spaces.

An autumn dawn breaks over the Lagan, a mist swirling softly above the green-grey water. A rosy glow enshrouds the figure of a tall, graceful woman, holding aloft a circle of peace, the world at her feet. At nightfall, blue neon lighting brings a surreal sheen to her steel-framed silhouette. Crossing the Queen's Bridge, by day or by night, it is impossible to escape the towering presence of Lady of Thanksgiving, one of many dramatic installations in the living gallery of contemporary art which Laganside Corporation has forged along the riverbank through its strategy of 'connecting art, people and place'.

From Kinney Design's colourful mosaic mural in Garmoyle Street, illustrating the heroic transatlantic voyage of St. Brendan, along to the sinuous, shell-like aluminium whirl of Ned Jackson Smyth's Homage to the Lagan on Stranmillis Embankment, water is the guiding force in a wealth of stories, vividly told in numerous pieces of public art.

On the cobbled quayside of Clarendon Dock, Vivien Burnside's gigantic bronze and stainless steel Dividers forms an archway, looking in one direction out to sea towards the Samson and Goliath cranes of Harland & Wolff and, in the other, into the bustling life of the city.

At Prince's Dock Street, Maurice Harron's The Flying Angel, a spiky bronze and stainless steel construction, rears up like the prow of a ship outside the Mission to Seafarers. The Angel is conceived as a protective force, calming the waves, and was inspired by a stirring verse from the Book of Revelations.

Underneath the parapets supporting the Lagan Bridge and surrounded by the thunder of traffic, Peter Rooney's Wheels of Progress tells smaller tales of a vanished community. Enclosed in frames in the shape of car mirrors are old photographs of families and school groups, graphics of tickets, passports and luggage labels, which take passers-by on quieter journeys back into another time. A poem scribbled on a postcard laments 'Where wander now those lost souls of Sailortown?'

Paddy McCann's powerful The Calling comes into its own at night, when a single shaft of light links two fibreglass figures atop lofty steel posts at the entrance to the Cathedral Quarter. Down below, the cast iron and brass coin bollards of Peter Rooney's Penny for Your Thoughts are engraved with reminders of the dealings which once took place within the quarter's narrow streets and courtyards – a bunch of bananas, a whiskey still, a flax flower, a pig, a cow and the city's founding father, Sir Arthur Chichester.

The inlaid stone slabs of Writers' Square pay tribute to Belfast's great writers, while the steel, copper and mosaic signage on the brick walls of Cotton Court is the creation of twelve artists working with community groups. One wall of the courtyard is occupied by Eleanor Wheeler's Mapping History, a collection of 1,200 tiles, personalised with artistic designs, messages of unrequited love – and even a marriage proposal. Its centrepiece is a relief of the Cathedral Quarter.

A section of Oxford Street is dominated by Rita Duffy's 'Dreams', a tapestry of aluminium panels, etched with portraits of children, whose dreams

LAGANSIDE CORPORATION

THE STORY SO FAR
A RIVER RUNS THROUGH IT
CHANGING THE FACE OF BELFAST
BUSINESS COMES BACK

A PLAYGROUND ON THE RIVER
MAKING OPPORTUNITIES FOR ALL
THE ART OF THE POSSIBLE
THROUGH THE EYES OF THE WORLD

GARDINER BROS EST 1855
JEWELLERS WARING ST

J M'GEE 42-46 HIGH ST
ULSTER GREATCOAT 1844

1941
BELFAST BLITZ

BELFAST POTTERY

Cathedral Quarter

VICTORIA STREET

FOUNDRY

HILL ST 1741

90.91

1   Outstretched arms of hope reach over the city
Thanksgiving Square art piece by Andy Scott

glow at night through back-lit glass panels. On Lanyon Place, Deborah Brown's bronze Sheep on the Road recalls the livestock markets of the Markets Area, while Susan Crowther's galvanised steel Lagan Symphony weaves together music and bird motifs in an eloquent fusion of the natural life of the river and the harmonies emanating from the Waterfront Hall.

The river meanders on to The Gasworks, to Eleanor Wheeler's sculpted brick piers and panels, Susan Crowther's undulating steel railings, Claire Sampson's sandstone columns and Mike Hogg's aluminium Bottle Top near the site of the old glass works. On the opposite bank, Jo-Ann Hatty's blue steel Porthole, fixes its beady eye on the distant shipyards.

And downriver on Donegall Quay lurks John Kindness's iconic Bigfish, a favourite location for tourist photographs and a symbol of celebration to the salmon, enticed back by the regenerated Lagan waters. Artfully constructed in shaded ceramic mosaic, it carries a myriad of images of Belfast ancient and modern.

The art of the possible has accomplished the seemingly impossible. Belfast has reclaimed the Lagan as its life-blood; its people have turned their faces back towards it; history has resurfaced, alive and ever-present. And the river flows on.

1 Wheels of Progress by Peter Rooney
2 Sheep on the Road by Deborah Brown
3 The Ulster Brewer by Ross Wilson
4 The Big Red by Catherine Harper

LAGANSIDE CORPORATION

THE STORY SO FAR
A RIVER RUNS THROUGH IT
CHANGING THE FACE OF BELFAST
BUSINESS COMES BACK

A PLAYGROUND ON THE RIVER
MAKING OPPORTUNITIES FOR ALL
THE ART OF THE POSSIBLE
THROUGH THE EYES OF THE WORLD

We've enjoyed a very real and fruitful partnership with Laganside Corporation since we contemplated our move to Cathedral Quarter some eight years ago. Laganside has literally put Belfast Community Circus on the map and, in turn, I believe we've added to what Cathedral Quarter has to offer.

Will Chamberlain, Belfast Community Circus

1 2 3 4

1   The Whirlpool at Custom House Square
2   Homage to the Lagan by Ned Jackson Smyth
3   Dividers by Vivien Burnside
4   Porthole by Jo-Ann Hatty

LAGANSIDE CORPORATION

THE STORY SO FAR
A RIVER RUNS THROUGH IT
CHANGING THE FACE OF BELFAST
BUSINESS COMES BACK

A PLAYGROUND ON THE RIVER
MAKING OPPORTUNITIES FOR ALL
THE ART OF THE POSSIBLE
THROUGH THE EYES OF THE WORLD

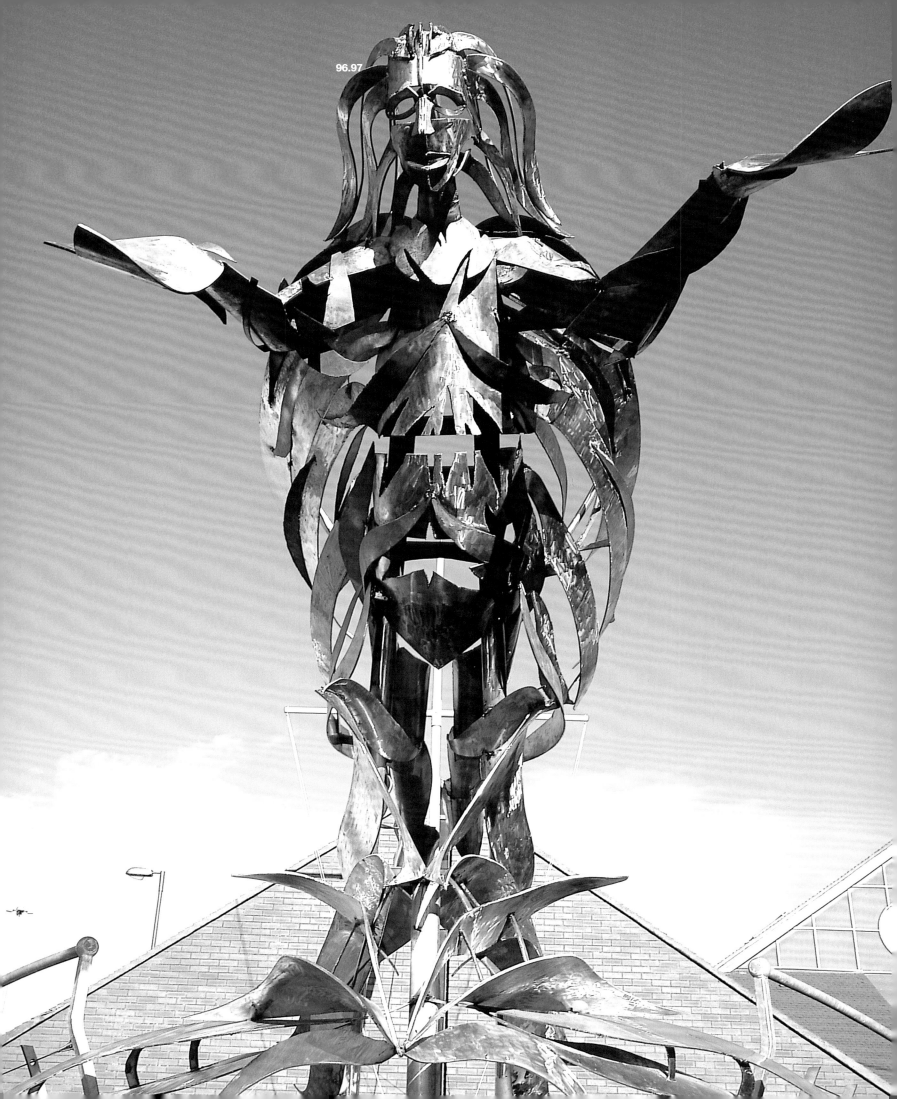

LAGANSIDE CORPORATION

THE STORY SO FAR
A RIVER RUNS THROUGH IT
CHANGING THE FACE OF BELFAST
BUSINESS COMES BACK

A PLAYGROUND ON THE RIVER
MAKING OPPORTUNITIES FOR ALL
THE ART OF THE POSSIBLE
THROUGH THE EYES OF THE WORLD

And I saw another angel fly in
the midst of heaven, having the
everlasting gospel to preach unto
them that dwell on the earth, and
to every nation, and kindred, and
tongue, and people.

Revelation Chapter 14, Verse 6

1 2

1 The Flying Angel by Maurice Harron
2 Starboard by Rachel Joynt

Life, spaces, buildings - in that order please.

Jan Gehl, Danish architect

1   2   1 Bigfish by John Kindness
              2 Bottle Top by Mike Hogg

LAGANSIDE CORPORATION

Through the eyes of the world

Greg Clark

1 Historic symbols of a bygone age reflected in the modern structures of a new era.

LAGANSIDE CORPORATION

THE STORY SO FAR
A RIVER RUNS THROUGH IT
CHANGING THE FACE OF BELFAST
BUSINESS COMES BACK

A PLAYGROUND ON THE RIVER
MAKING OPPORTUNITIES FOR ALL
THE ART OF THE POSSIBLE
THROUGH THE EYES OF THE WORLD

The Organisation for Economic Co-operation and Development (OECD) is a unique forum of 30 countries working together to address the economic, social and environmental challenges of globalisation. The OECD has twice reported on the work of Laganside Corporation, providing valuable external assessments of its achievements and drawing lessons for other agencies, cities, regions and governments around the world.

Belfast is no ordinary place in which to undertake urban regeneration, and yet making Belfast an ordinary modern compact capital city was part of the task.

The regeneration of the banks of the River Lagan and associated urban locations in Belfast over an 18 year period from 1989 to 2007 will be seen in the future as a remarkable effort of faith and discipline.

It is hard to imagine the starting point these days. Back in 1986 when the idea was first mooted people literally laughed. It was impossible to undertake regeneration because the context was so hostile and uncertain. The idea of regeneration assumed that a market for investment in the city could be re-established and that confidence could be engendered through practical local initiative.

Despite the tough beginnings and systemic cynicism, the Laganside Corporation was born and set about its task with some considerable patience and vigour.

Many lessons were learned on the way.

Laganside Corporation shows us the importance of getting the right phases and sequences in urban regeneration; how to plan, undertake infrastructure development and environmental improvements, how to attract investors and create new place destinations, and to build community engagement and benefit. None of these are easy, but to make regeneration work they have to be sequenced together carefully.

The result in Belfast has been a vastly improved riverside area with new centre city living and many modern amenities. Jobs and investment have been attracted in large numbers, drawn by the new infrastructure, high quality public realm, and amenities.

The centre of Belfast as a whole has benefited too, with a new investor confidence in the whole of the city, and many wider regeneration projects are now underway in the central core and along the rest of the waterfront.

Belfast is better positioned as result to be the capital that Northern Ireland needs, offering a modernised city with the capacity to host the modern functions of a small capital in an open knowledge-based economy.

Viewing the achievements of Laganside Corporation from this lens of 'concentric circles' enables us to see that the regeneration of a small area of central Belfast has much wider benefits and impacts, in part because the Lagan

was where the history of Belfast began, and the years of development that followed were built on the relationships to this central place. Thus, as the centre is regenerated it can occasion a re-calibration of the whole local and regional economy.

This insight points to the importance of maintaining a clear plan and strategy for the continued redevelopment of the city as a whole and the wider metropolitan area. These wider processes of regeneration and redevelopment may also need much of the careful and orchestrated handling that Laganside Corporation was able to provide to the redevelopment of the Lagan.

Laganside Corporation has done its job. The area for which it was responsible will not require fundamental regeneration again for at least 50 years. Those who have played their part in delivering this intervention to create a new future for Belfast deserve to be recognised and credited for the success. It has taken no small

effort, and has benefited from decisive leadership and capable professionalism.

At the heart of the regeneration has been the building of trust and confidence in a different kind of future for Belfast. Trust was essential to make the initial investments and plans, and to attempt to deliver them. Confidence has been the result and the oil that has made the rest possible.

There is a wider task now at hand; the imperative to regenerate the whole city and to re-fortify its role as the central engine in the regional economy. The fact that this is now the compelling task is recognition of the success of Laganside Corporation in bringing the city to this juncture.

Let us not forget that this was a task that many thought impossible.

LAGANSIDE CORPORATION

THE STORY SO FAR
A RIVER RUNS THROUGH IT
CHANGING THE FACE OF BELFAST
BUSINESS COMES BACK

A PLAYGROUND ON THE RIVER
MAKING OPPORTUNITIES FOR ALL
THE ART OF THE POSSIBLE
THROUGH THE EYES OF THE WORLD

1   2

1   BBC Radio Ulster's 30th birthday celebrations in Custom House Square
2   International business flourishes on the waterfront

LAGANSIDE CORPORATION

THE STORY SO FAR
A RIVER RUNS THROUGH IT
CHANGING THE FACE OF BELFAST
BUSINESS COMES BACK

A PLAYGROUND ON THE RIVER
MAKING OPPORTUNITIES FOR ALL
THE ART OF THE POSSIBLE
THROUGH THE EYES OF THE WORLD

Laganside Corporation has returned the river to the city and demonstrated what can be achieved through inclusive, focused partnership. The challenge for the city now is to build on and sustain its legacy.

Peter McNaney, Chief Executive, Belfast City Council

1 2 3

1 The Odyssey complex - providing entertainment for all
2 The headquarters of Laganside Corporation at Clarendon Dock
3 Apartment living, right in the city centre

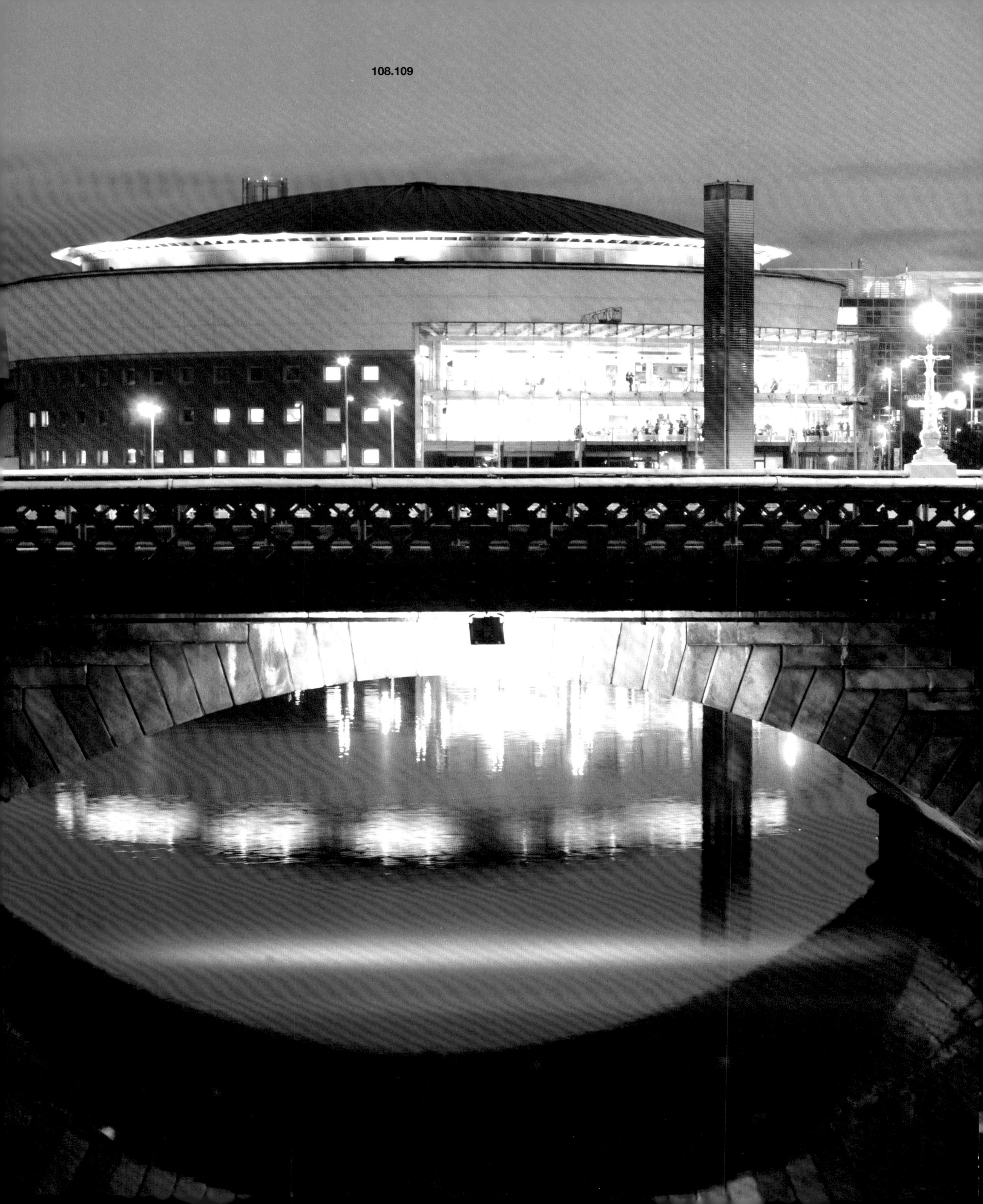

LAGANSIDE CORPORATION

THE STORY SO FAR
A RIVER RUNS THROUGH IT
CHANGING THE FACE OF BELFAST
BUSINESS COMES BACK

A PLAYGROUND ON THE RIVER
MAKING OPPORTUNITIES FOR ALL
THE ART OF THE POSSIBLE
THROUGH THE EYES OF THE WORLD

1   2

1 A shining example of regeneration
2 Old makes new in Cathedral Quarter

Contributing to the revitalisation of Belfast and Northern Ireland by transforming Laganside to be attractive, accessible and sustainable, recognised as a place of opportunity for all.

Laganside Corporation Mission Statement

LAGANSIDE CORPORATION

THE STORY SO FAR
A RIVER RUNS THROUGH IT
CHANGING THE FACE OF BELFAST
BUSINESS COMES BACK

A PLAYGROUND ON THE RIVER
MAKING OPPORTUNITIES FOR ALL
THE ART OF THE POSSIBLE
THROUGH THE EYES OF THE WORLD

1   Open spaces between buildings
2   Thousands tour the cleaned-up river every year
3   Connecting the new to the old in Cathedral Quarter
4   The Halifax contact centre towers over the new Gasworks hub

1 The award winning Bar Library blends the new with Belfast's past
2 Reflecting the past - the restored Meter House at the Gasworks

LAGANSIDE CORPORATION

THE STORY SO FAR
A RIVER RUNS THROUGH IT
CHANGING THE FACE OF BELFAST
BUSINESS COMES BACK

A PLAYGROUND ON THE RIVER
MAKING OPPORTUNITIES FOR ALL
THE ART OF THE POSSIBLE
THROUGH THE EYES OF THE WORLD

1 The end of a working day on the new riverfront

LAGANSIDE CORPORATION

THE STORY SO FAR
A RIVER RUNS THROUGH IT
CHANGING THE FACE OF BELFAST
BUSINESS COMES BACK

A PLAYGROUND ON THE RIVER
MAKING OPPORTUNITIES FOR ALL
THE ART OF THE POSSIBLE
THROUGH THE EYES OF THE WORLD

1989

1	2
3	4
5	6

1 The disused and undervalued River Lagan
2 Belfast Gasworks prior to redevelopment
3 Clarendon Dock as a working quayside

4 Lanyon Place when it was just a car park
5 The Odyssey site was once coal quays
6 Cotton Court was a derelict part of Waring Street

LAGANSIDE CORPORATION

THE STORY SO FAR
A RIVER RUNS THROUGH IT
CHANGING THE FACE OF BELFAST
BUSINESS COMES BACK

A PLAYGROUND ON THE RIVER
MAKING OPPORTUNITIES FOR ALL
THE ART OF THE POSSIBLE
THROUGH THE EYES OF THE WORLD

2007

1	2
3	4
5	6

1 A refreshed River Lagan
2 The Gasworks - home to international companies
3 Clarendon Dock - a new business district

4 Lanyon Place - icon of waterfront Belfast
5 The Millennium Odyssey project
6 Donegall Street in the revitalised Cathedral Quarter

Laganside
Corporation Chairmen,
Board Members and
Chief Executives
1989 - 2007

Chairmen

Duke of Abercorn	1989 - 1996
Anthony S Hopkins	1997 - 2007

Board Members

Duke of Abercorn	1989 - 1996
John B McGuckian	1989 - 1991
Dr Brian Feeney	1989 - 1995
Jim Fitzpatrick	1989 - 1995
John Carson	1989 - 1991
Fred Cobain	1989 - 2001
Mrs Margaret Spence	1989 - 1995
Dr Brum Henderson	1989 - 1991
Dawson Moreland	1989 - 1990
Gordon Irwin	1990 - 2004
Ernest Airey	1992 - 1998
Dr Lucinda Blackiston-Houston	1992 - 1998
Sir Reg Empey	1992 - 1998
Joseph Jaworski	1992 - 1994
Dr Alisdair McDonnell	1994 - 2001
Anthony S Hopkins	1995 - 2007
Mrs Rona Fairhead	1995 - 1998
Ms Geraldine McAteer	1995 - 2007
Hugh Smith	1998 - 1999
George Priestley	1998 - 2007
Ms Ann Marie Slavin	1998 - 2007
Ms Jayne Morrice	1998 - 2007
Mrs Lucy Woods	1998 - 1999
Robert Stoker	2002 - 2005
Colm Bradley	2001 - 2007
Sammy Douglas	2001 - 2007
Chris Kane	2001 - 2007
John Doran	2004 - 2005
Ian Crozier	2005 - 2007
Roy Adair	2006 - 2007

Chief Executives

George Mackey	1989 - 1998
Mike Smith	1998 - 2002
Kyle Alexander	2002 - 2007

Staff who served Laganside for more than 15 years

Mike Smith
Kyle Alexander
David McCracken
Susan Quail
Clive Graham
Marie Louise Lappin
Ciara Barnes

LAGANSIDE CORPORATION

THE STORY SO FAR
A RIVER RUNS THROUGH IT
CHANGING THE FACE OF BELFAST
BUSINESS COMES BACK

A PLAYGROUND ON THE RIVER
MAKING OPPORTUNITIES FOR ALL
THE ART OF THE POSSIBLE
THROUGH THE EYES OF THE WORLD

Contributors

Alan Watson
Alan is a former business and political journalist now working in public relations.

Peter Hunter and Bill Morrison
Peter, a visionary London architect, jointly authored the original Laganside Concept Plan and was architectural advisor to the Laganside Corporation Board. Bill is a planning consultant who was Divisional Planning Officer in Belfast during the 1990s.

Charlie Warmington
Charlie is a freelance journalist and broadcaster presently on commission to the Lagan Legacy charitable maritime heritage organisation.

James Stinson
James is a business journalist currently on the staff of the Irish News.

Ian Hill
Ian is an author, social diarist, cultural commentator and travel writer whose publications include the Insight Guide to Belfast. Among his public appointments are memberships of the Historic Buildings Council and the Board of the Cathedral Quarter Arts Festival.

Kyle Alexander and David Lockhart
Kyle was Laganside Corporation's Chief Executive from 2002 until 2007. David owns a training and development company and acted as Employment and Employability consultant to Laganside Corporation

Jane Coyle
Jane is an award-winning arts journalist, writer and critic.

Greg Clark
Greg is Chair of the Organisation for Economic Co-operation and Development's LEED (Local Economic and Employment Development) Forum of Cities and Regions, and an advisor to the UK government.

Photography
Brian Morrison Photography / Rory Moore Photography / Christopher Hill Photographic
Harrison Photography / Esler Crawford Photography / Zirkus / John Boucher

LAGANSIDE

LAGANSIDE: OUR LEGACY, YOUR FUTURE